Basic
Pottery Making

Basic Pottery Making

A Complete Guide

Linda Franz, editor

*Mark Fitzgerald,
potter and consultant*

*photographs by
Jason Minick*

STACKPOLE
BOOKS
Essex, Connecticut
Blue Ridge Summit, Pennsylvania

Thanks to Mark Fitzgerald for sharing his expertise and pottery designs and for allowing us to use his workshop. Thanks also to Huynh Mai Fitzgerald for her help and support.

Thanks to Jason Minick for his wonderful photos.

And thanks to Mark Allison, Janelle Steen, and all the folks at Stackpole Books who helped put this book together.

STACKPOLE BOOKS

An imprint of Globe Pequot, the trade division of
The Rowman & Littlefield Publishing Group, Inc.
4501 Forbes Blvd., Ste. 200
Lanham, MD 20706
www.rowman.com

Distributed by NATIONAL BOOK NETWORK

Copyright © 2009 by Stackpole Books

We have made every effort to ensure the accuracy and completeness of these instructions. We cannot, however, be responsible for human error, typographical mistakes, or variations in individual work.

British Library Cataloguing in Publication Information available

Previously cataloged with the Library of Congress as follows:

Basic pottery making : all the skills and tools you need to get started / Linda Franz, editor ; Mark Fitzgerald, potter and consultant ; photographs by Jason Minick. — 1st ed.
    p. cm.
 ISBN-13: 978-0-8117-3531-5
 ISBN-10: 0-8117-3531-1
 1. Pottery craft. I. Franz, Linda. II. Fitzgerald, Mark.
 TT920.B355 2009
 738.1—dc22

                                                        2008023591

ISBN: 978-0-8117-7137-5 (paper : alk.)
ISBN: 978-0-8117-7138-2 (ebook)

♾™ The paper used in this publication meets the minimum requirements of American National Standard for Information Sciences—Permanence of Paper for Printed Library Materials, ANSI/NISO Z39.48-1992.

Contents

Introduction

This book offers detailed instructions on how to throw a clay pot on a pottery wheel. All of the projects described are thrown on a wheel.

Throwing a pot is a skill that takes practice. By following the step-by-step instructions given here, you'll learn how to pull up and shape a pot. You'll learn how to trim it, fire it, and glaze it. Through practice, you'll learn how to add the right amount of water as you throw a pot, and your fingers will feel when the pot has reached the proper thickness.

You'll start with some basic skills that will be needed in every project, beginning with how to wedge clay. Then you'll throw a simple bowl. Next, you'll make mugs in three different shapes by throwing off a mound. You'll learn how to shape and attach a pulled handle to each mug. For the final project, a sugar bowl and creamer set, you'll learn how to make a spout and a lidded bowl.

After learning how to bisque fire your pieces, you'll learn how to glaze the pots using a dip and pour method to add two colors of glaze to some pieces and three colors of glaze to others. A glaze firing will complete the projects.

Use your creativity and the skills that you learn in this book to create your own unique stoneware.

Let's begin.

1

Tools and Equipment

A pottery or ceramic supplier will carry all the premixed clay, glaze, tools, and equipment needed to make pottery. Check your local yellow pages to find a supplier near you. The Internet is another good source to find companies that sell equipment and supplies and a good way to compare prices.

Often, many of the small pottery-making tools can be purchased together as a kit. Don't worry if the kit you see includes a slightly different potter's rib or modeling tool than the ones shown in this book. They'll do the job just as well.

By far the most expensive pieces of equipment needed to make pottery are a pottery wheel and a kiln. If you're not yet ready to buy your own kiln, kiln space can sometimes be rented at local pottery businesses or ceramic suppliers. Ask a manager if this might be possible.

Buying a Pottery Wheel

Pottery wheels cost from about $500 to more than $1,500 for heavy-duty models. They can be purchased from a local ceramic supplier or from an online supplier. The advantage to purchasing locally is that you can see the wheel before you purchase it, and you'll pay no shipping costs. You may, however, find more choices online, and some online suppliers also offer free shipping.

Most wheels are electric-powered with a foot pedal that controls the speed. Some models have a foot pedal that is attached to the wheel rather than attached by an electrical cord. This can limit mobility. Choose a wheel that has a motor of at least ¼ horsepower. A less powerful motor will limit the type of pieces you can create.

Most pottery wheels have legs and are free-standing. Some have leg extensions so that you can raise or lower the wheel. If you want to work in a standing position, purchase a wheel with leg extensions. Tabletop wheels are also available.

SPLASH PAN
This pottery wheel has a two-piece splash pan to catch the water and mud that fly off a wheel in use. Wheels are often sold with splash pans included, but sometimes the pan must be purchased separately. In either case, a splash pan is essential for keeping a neat and clean workplace.

SCALE
A household scale can be used to measure 1- and 5-pound weights of clay for your projects.

CHAMOIS
A small piece of chamois is moistened and used to smooth the rims of pots.

BAT

The bat is placed on the potter's wheel and is the surface on which you'll make your pots. About a dozen bats will be needed because some pots must remain on the bat until they dry. While many types of bats are available to purchase, this bat was made by the potter from particleboard. Bats made of plastic or particleboard are relatively inexpensive choices. Some plastic bats may not be as rigid as those made of particleboard. Note the two small holes near the edge of the bat. The holes are placed over pins on the wheel to hold the bat in place.

SPONGE

A good sponge that fits in your hand is essential in making pots. It is used to add water and soak up excess water while you are throwing pots and to shape and smooth them. Later you'll use your sponge to clean glaze from waxed areas of the pots. The sponge on the left is synthetic. A natural elephant ear sponge is shown on the right.

BAT LIFTER

Can be used instead of the fettling knife to pry and lift the bat from the wheel.

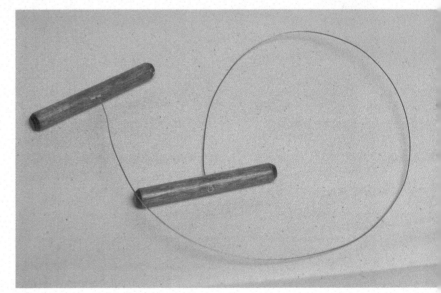

WIRE CLAY CUTTERS

Use the wire clay cutters to cut blocks of clay into smaller portions and to cut completed pots from the wheel.

POTTER'S RIB WITH SERRATED EDGE
This tool is used for feathering. It gives the pot texture.

METAL RIBS
These tools, in a variety of sizes, are used for smoothing, scraping, and shaping the pot while it's still on the wheel.

WOODEN POTTER'S RIB
Use this tool to shape pots.

WOODEN MODELING TOOL
Used to add grooves or other markings to clay. It can be used both when the clay is wet and at the leather-hard stage.

CUTTING TOOL
The cutting tool is used to remove excess clay from pots before they are removed from the wheel.

LOOP TOOL
This tool is used to shape and cut away excess clay from the pot at the leather-hard stage.

TRIMMING TOOL
Used to trim and shape the pot at the leather-hard stage.

NEEDLE TOOL
Also called a pin tool, this piece has a few uses. You can check the thickness of pot bottoms with it to determine if they're too thick or too thin. It's also sometimes used to cut clay.

FETTLING KNIFE
Use the fettling knife to cut pulled handles into lengths. It can also be used to lift bats from the pottery wheel.

CRAFT KNIFE
Used to cut away small pieces of clay to create slots and other openings.

3-INCH PUTTY KNIFE
After completing one pot, use the putty knife to clean clay from the bat before making another pot.

CALIPERS
Used to measure the diameter of an opening or piece of clay so that the diameter can be transferred to a corresponding feature.

Buying a Kiln

Both electric and gas kilns are available, but electric kilns are less expensive, easier to use, and usually have fewer firing problems. Kiln prices begin at about $1,200 to $1,500 and can cost several thousand dollars for larger ones. They can be purchased from a local ceramic supplier or online.

You must always use a circuit that has the same voltage and the same or higher amperage rating than the kiln requires. If you have 20 amps available and you need 30 amps, you will first need an electrician. Kilns generally require 208- or 240-volt service. Make sure to check that the voltage matches the electric service available.

The kiln you choose must fire hot enough for the pottery you intend to make, and most experts recommend purchasing a kiln that fires hotter than you need because with age, kilns fire to a lower temperature. To fire cone 6, choose a kiln that can fire cone 8 or 10.

If you are a hobbyist, choose a kiln of at least 2.5 cubic feet. If you plan to make lots of pottery, choose a larger kiln. Even the smallest of kilns generally can accommodate more than one level of pottery for firing. At the

time you purchase your kiln, you can also purchase kiln "furniture." This consists of posts in varying heights that support full or half shelves. The posts and shelves are made of a ceramic brick material.

A vent for your kiln is essential if you are firing in an attached garage or other space that is connected to your house or other living quarters. Venting removes odors and unsafe fumes.

For more information on choosing a kiln, check out the website www.hotkilns.com.

CLAY

Moist clay can be purchased as two 25-pound blocks in a 50-pound box. Clay must be stored in a plastic bag to keep from drying out before you're ready to use it.

Stoneware clay is the best clay to use for functional pottery because it is the densest and strongest. Choose a stoneware clay that can be fired to cone 6. The "cone" rating is an indication of temperature that includes firing time. The clay will be at its hardest and densest when fired to cone 6.

GLAZE

Premixed glaze is used to give color and a finished coat to pots. Kilns are fired not just to a temperature but to a "cone" level, which includes time as well as temperature. A faster heating rate will require a slightly higher temperature than a slower heating rate. Purchase dinnerware-safe glaze that can be fired to cone 5 or 6.

BRUSHES

Small brushes are used to apply wax to areas of the pot that shouldn't be glazed.

WAX

Ready-to-use liquid wax can be purchased from a pottery supplier. It is used to coat areas of the bisque-fired pot that should not be glazed.

Containers for water and glazes, an old towel, a ruler, and glaze-stirring sticks are also needed to make pottery.

2

Basic Skills

Before you begin to throw a pot on the wheel, you'll need to master a few basic skills. Wedging the clay is the most important of these and will help you immeasurably when you work on the wheel. Reusing clay, making slip, and determining the thickness of pieces are also fundamental skills.

Basic Skills

Clay must be prepared for throwing by "wedging" it on a sturdy work surface; the wedging process is similar to kneading dough for bread. Clay is made up of millions of particles. Wedging the clay not only gets the air out, it also aligns the particles so the clay is easier to work.

1. Use a clean hardwood surface for wedging. Begin by pushing a piece of clay forward and down with your right hand.

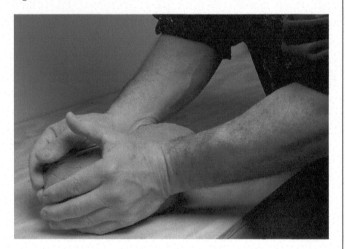

2. Pull the clay back with your left hand.

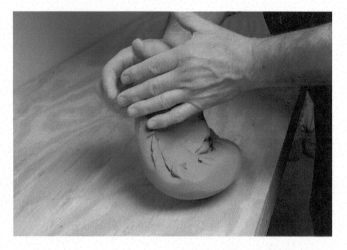

The clay will spiral as you work it.

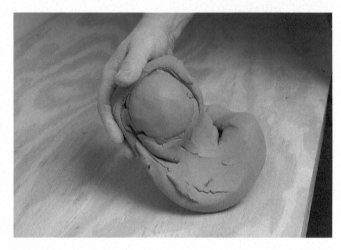

3. Continue to wedge the clay by pushing it forward with your right hand and pulling it back with your left hand.

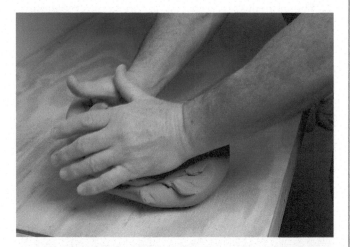

4. Complete fifty to eighty wedging repetitions to prepare the clay for throwing. It requires practice to wedge clay and to know when it has been wedged enough.

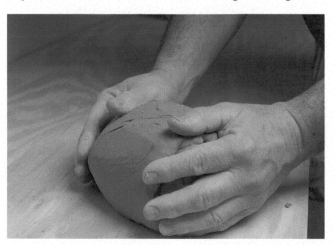

Note: Clay cannot be wedged too much, but it can be wedged incorrectly. If you encounter air bubbles or uneven consistency, you've wedged it improperly or not enough. Try again.

5. The final step is to shape the clay into a cone by lifting the back and shaping the top into a point.

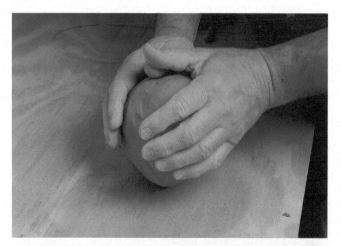

Basic Skills

11

Every potter generates plenty of scraps of clay while making pieces. The potter who is just learning usually adds more clay to the recycle heap than to the kiln as he or she figures out how to shape and distribute clay evenly from the bottom to the top of a pot. But don't despair about those failed pots and other scraps of clay that start to pile up around your wheel. Until clay is fired, it can be reclaimed and reused.

1. To begin the process of reclaiming used clay, keep a clean bat on the floor next to your wheel. Whenever you make a scrap of clay, or a whole pot must be scrapped, drop it onto the bat.

Tip: Scraps of clay trimmed from leather-hard pots can be reused as slip. Place them on a separate bat.

2. The more evenly your clay is spread out, the more evenly it will dry. Shape the clay into a disk with your hands.

3. Place the clay back on the bat and flatten it somewhat. Set it aside and let the clay dry for a few hours until it gets to the same dryness it was when you started to throw it. When it reaches that dryness, place it in a plastic bag to keep it from drying further. The clay must be wedged before it can be used again.

The creamy clay solution called slip is used to decorate pots before firing and also as a glue to attach handles or other pieces of clay to your pots. It's easy to make your own slip—and it's another good use for clay scraps.

1. First gather some dried scraps of clay.

2. Add the clay scraps to a small container of water.

3. Let the clay sit in the water overnight.

4. Stir until smooth.

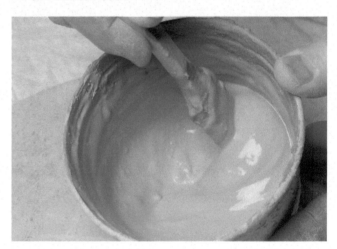

5. Add enough water so that when you're finished, the slip is the same consistency as heavy cream. If your slip is too wet, add more pieces of dried clay and let it sit overnight. Stir until smooth. This uncolored slip will be used to attach handles.

Basic Skills

13

To make a light brown slip, you'll add rutile, which is a mineral.

1. For 1 cup of slip, add 2 tablespoons of rutile and stir.

2. Now add 1½ teaspoons of red iron oxide. Rutile and red iron oxide can be purchased from a pottery supplier.

3. Stir in the iron oxide, and your light brown slip is ready to use.

To make a darker brown slip, you'll use red iron oxide alone.

1. Add 2 tablespoons of red iron oxide to 1 cup of slip and stir.

Now the dark brown slip is ready. Colored slip can be used to decorate pots before they are fired. The area you decorate will differ from the rest of the pot after it is glazed and fired.

Equipment Setup

Throwing pots is a messy task that takes a bit of space. A garage or workshop is a good space in which to set up your pottery wheel and other equipment. Many potters wear a full-length apron when working. Plan on getting dirty from head to foot and dress accordingly. Keeping tools, a pan of water, and an old towel nearby will help you as you work at the wheel.

Basic Skills

Beginning potters can use a couple of techniques to determine the thickness of a pot.

A needle tool is a good tool to determine the thickness of the bottom of a pot.

1. To use it, push the point into the bottom of the pot until it touches the bat.

2. Place your index finger on the needle and the surface of the clay, without pressing the clay.

3. Keeping your finger in place, pull out the needle. The length of needle between the tip and your finger matches the thickness of the clay. Measure it with a ruler. The bottom of this bowl is about ½ inch thick, a sturdy thickness.

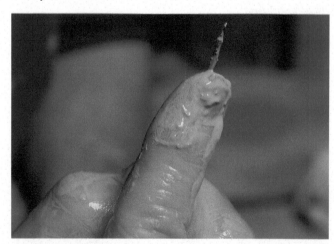

Note: If you are concerned that your pots aren't balanced or are too thick, you can cut one in half using the wire clay cutter. Although the pot will be ruined, it can help you determine on which areas you need to work with future pots.

The sides of this mug measure about ¼ inch thick near the bottom and taper slightly before thickening at the rim. If a pot is too thin, it will collapse. But a thick pot takes longer to dry and is heavy when it is complete.

3

Making a Bowl

Making a simple bowl is an excellent way to learn the basics of throwing a pot on a wheel. The skills required are few, but it will take a while to master them. Fortunately, you can easily reuse the clay from projects that don't come out the way you want. When you're successful, you'll have a beautiful and useful handcrafted piece of pottery.

Forming the Bowl

To begin, you'll use a scale to weigh a 5-pound block of clay, which will be made into one bowl.

1. Take the equivalent of several handfuls of clay from the container.

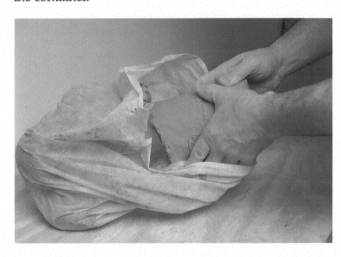

Tip: Remember that when you're not working it, clay must be kept in a plastic bag or container so it stays moist.

2. Place the clay on the scale.

3. Cut off some of the clay with a wire clay cutter to get it to 5 pounds.

4. Wedge the clay to prepare it for throwing. Repeat the wedging motions fifty to eighty times, then form the clay into a cone.

5. Secure the bat onto your wheel by placing the openings on the bat over the pins on the wheel head.

6. Place a plastic pan of water close to your wheel. Use a sponge to wet the bat. Wetting the bat helps hold the clay in place. Turn on the wheel to a slow speed and wet the bat from the inside to the outside. The bat is now ready for the clay.

7. Turn off the wheel. Put the cone of clay onto the bat as close to the center as you can.

8. Flatten the clay slightly.

9. Wet your sponge in the pan of water and turn on the wheel to a fast speed.

10. Position your hands in the exact center of the wheel and form a circle with them that the clay can conform to so that it doesn't wobble. Centering the clay is a skill that requires practice and can be difficult for a beginning potter to master.

11. Holding the sponge in your right hand, use it to wet the clay as you gently squeeze in on the clay and center it.

12. Because you are using a fairly large amount of clay, you will want to shape the clay into a low disk form. Use your thumbs to begin flattening the clay. Put your thumbs in the center of the top and pull them to the outside, stretching the clay while it is turning. At the same time, use your fingers to keep the disk centered.

13. Flatten the clay further by pressing it gently with the heel of your hand. Now the clay should be centered on the wheel. The clay is centered when it no longer wobbles.

14. Keep the sponge in your right hand as you work, and use it to keep the clay moist.

15. Open the pot by pushing down inside with your left hand in the exact center and pulling up the wall with your right hand outside the pot. Keep the wheel at a moderate speed while pulling up. Be careful not to push down too deep.

The opening and first pull up is all one move with the left hand inside and the right hand outside.

16. Continue the first pull up.

17. After each pull, push down on the lip of the bowl with your fingers to keep it from getting too thin. Use your sponge to wet the bowl during each pull. When water collects inside the bowl, wick it away with the sponge. The bowl becomes too wet if moisture accumulates in the bottom.

18. Generally, a bowl of this size should be pulled up three times from the bottom to the top. It will take practice to pull up a bowl in three tries. Each time, as you're moving up the bowl, apply more pressure from inside the bowl to flare it.

The bowl quickly takes shape. Your goal in pulling up is to distribute the clay as evenly as you can from top to bottom. The sides of the bowl should gradually taper in thickness from about ½ inch at the bottom of the bowl to ¼ inch at the top before thickening again at the lip.

19. Stop the wheel and measure the thickness of the bottom of the bowl with a needle tool. It should be about ½ inch thick.

20. Now shape the bowl three to four times with the wheel on a moderate to slow speed. With one hand inside and the other hand outside the bowl, press the clay between your fingers from the bottom of the bowl to the top. To make the bowl flare out, apply more pressure with your inside hand. It will take practice to achieve the shape you desire. Use the sponge to wet the bowl. Keep a sheen of water on the surface so the pot moves smoothly between your hands.

21. Use a wet chamois to smooth the lip of the bowl.

22. Next you'll clean out the bottom of the bowl and curve it using a small metal rib.

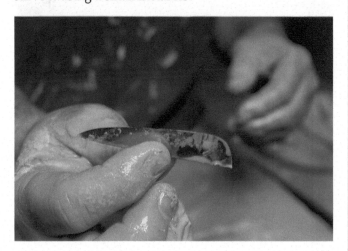

23. With the wheel on a moderate speed, point the narrow end of the rib toward the middle of the bowl and use the profile of the rib to shape the bottom.

24. Shape the bottom of the bowl from the center to the edge. Shape it about three times, cleaning the rib after each shaping.

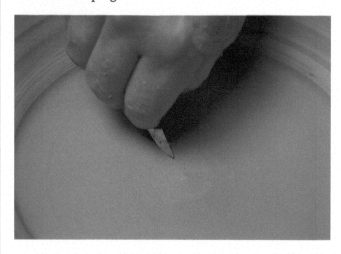

25. After your final pass with the rib, use the sponge to refine the inside shape.

26. Use the wet chamois to smooth the rim of the bowl so there is no unevenness.

27. Press with your index finger through the sponge to create a swirl in the bottom of the bowl. This decorative touch adds interest to the finished bowl.

28. Move your finger from the center of the bowl to the outside, as though you were dragging a needle across a spinning record on a turntable.

29. With the wheel on a slow speed, use a modeling tool to cut a decorative groove on the inside of the bowl just below the rim.

30. Wet the sponge and use it to smooth the groove you've just cut.

31. With the wheel rotating at a slow speed, remove excess clay from the base of the bowl with a cutting tool.

32. Use the wire cutter to cut the bowl from the bat. Keep the wire close to the bat and pull it through the clay toward you while the wheel is off.

33. Use the bat lifter to lift off the bat with the bowl still on it, and set it aside to dry to the leather-hard stage.

Tip: Depending on humidity, drying to the leather-hard stage can take from several hours to a few days. The pot must dry enough so it holds its shape when you handle it; it will still have enough moisture so you can trim it and attach handles. Once a pot has reached the leather-hard stage, you must move on to the finishing steps or cover the pot with plastic to keep it from drying further.

1. After the bowl is leather-hard, place another bat on top of it with the working side of the bat on the lip of the bowl, then lift the bowl by holding the bottom bat.

2. With one hand on each bat, flip the bowl so it is upside down. Secure the bottom bat onto the wheel.

3. Carefully remove the top bat from the bowl.

4. Now you're ready to trim the bowl. You'll use the tap method to center it on the bat. With the wheel on medium speed, tap the bowl as it spins at the part farthest out of center. Continue lightly tapping the bowl until it is centered and no longer wobbles.

5. Wet your sponge and, with the wheel at medium speed, moisten the edge of the bat, then turn off the wheel.

6. To secure the bowl to the bat, use three pieces of clay pushed down into the bat and onto the bowl's rim.

The three pieces of clay will hold the bowl in place.

You'll use a loop tool to do the trimming.

Tip: The loop tool needs to be held firmly enough so that a thin layer of clay peels away, but not so firmly that the tool gouges and ruins the bowl. The beginning potter will need to use trial and error to determine the amount to be trimmed.

7. With the wheel spinning at a moderate to high speed, use a loop tool to trim away excess clay. Point the narrow end of the loop tool to the bottom of the bowl. Trim upward from the bottom third of the bowl to establish a foot platform for the bottom of the bowl.

With more trimming, the foot platform emerges.

Excess clay can be trimmed from the base to the lip of the bowl.

8. Trim clay from the edge of the foot platform.

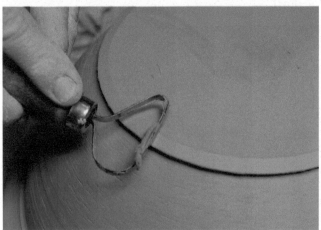

9. With the wheel spinning slowly, add a decorative ring to the bottom of the bowl using the moistened tip of a modeling tool.

10. Use the wet sponge to smooth the ring and the base of the bowl.

11. Potters often use a stamp to mark their creations. With the wheel turned off, stamp the bottom of the bowl or simply add your initials using a pin tool.

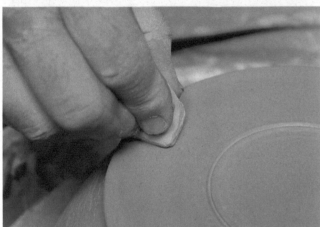

12. Once the bowl is stamped, remove the pieces of clay holding it to the bat, remove the bat from the wheel, and set the bowl aside on the bat to dry further until it's ready to be bisque fired. Drying will take from two days to a week.

Note: Bisque firing, glazing, and glaze firing are best done with several pieces at the same time. Those processes are therefore covered in chapter 6.

Making a Bowl

4

Making Mugs

In this chapter, you'll learn how to make three different styles
of mugs by "throwing off" a mound. One large piece of clay
can be used to make several mugs. Each style uses a hand-
pulled handle made separately and attached to the mug with
slip. You can make all three of the different styles or choose
the one you like best and make several mugs of the same style.

You will learn how to make a tall belled mug, a shorter belled mug, and a straight-edged mug. You will then learn how to make two different styles of pulled handles. As you perfect your pottery-making skills, you can combine different types of mugs and handles to create your own unique pieces.

In general, clay is centered and shaped with the wheel at a high speed. The mugs are pulled up with the wheel at a moderate speed, then shaped with the wheel at a moderate to slow speed.

Style 1

1. The first step is to wedge a piece of clay that weighs from 6 to 8 pounds, and then cone it.

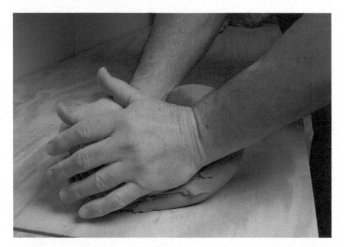

2. Place a bat on your wheel and wet it with your sponge. Put the clay in the middle of the wheel, getting it as close to the center as possible.

3. With the wheel on high speed, use your hands to center and shape the clay while it turns.

4. Use your sponge to wet the clay. Begin moving your hands up and down the clay, making the mound higher and narrower.

5. Cup your hands and grab a piece of clay about the size of an apple, keeping it attached to the clay mound. This is what you'll use to make your first mug.

6. With the wheel rotating at a moderate speed, cup your hands around the clay and put your right thumb in the exact center of the top of the clay to open it and spread it out.

7. After opening the pot, put two fingers of your left hand inside and the left thumb outside for the first pull. Wet the outside of the pot with your sponge and use the same amount of pressure from the inside and the outside to pull up evenly from the bottom to the top to a height of 3 to 4 inches.

8. As you pull up, take the sponge and "horseshoe" it over the top, pushing down slightly to thicken the lip. Keep the wheel at a moderate speed. Use the sponge to remove excess water as it accumulates in the bottom of the pot. At the same time, a little water must be added to the sides with each pull so they don't become too dry.

9. For the second pull, put your entire left hand in the pot to spread it apart and shape it. Apply pressure to the outside with your right hand while your left hand begins shaping from the inside.

Tip: Water that sits in a pot will weaken it, so water must continually be sponged out.

10. Create the width at the bottom of the mug by applying a little more pressure with your right hand.

11. After about three pulls, shape the mug three or four times from bottom to top, keeping the wheel at a moderate to slow speed. The mug is shaped by applying more pressure with your inside hand to start the outward curve. Apply more pressure from your outside hand to bring the curve inward. Reverse pressure again to widen the mug at the top.

12. With the wheel at a moderate speed, use the sponge to moisten the outside of the mug.

13. Use the wet chamois to smooth the lip of the mug.

14. With the wheel at a moderate to slow speed, use a cutting tool to begin to separate the mug from the clay mound. Carefully cut away clay below the base of the mug to separate it.

15. With the wheel off, use the wire clay cutter to finish cutting the mug from the clay mound by pulling from the outside of the mug base toward yourself.

16. Carefully remove the mug and set it aside to dry to the leather-hard stage (see tip on page 28).

17. Your mound of clay should yield about five mugs. When you've used up all the clay, clean off your bat with a 3-inch putty knife.

18. Scrape the clay from the bat with your putty knife while the wheel rotates slowly. Hold the putty knife nearly flat to the wheel while the wheel spins toward the knife.

Now you're ready to add another cone of clay and begin with the second mug shape, which is shorter with a smaller handle.

Style 2

1. With the wheel at a high speed, work the clay up and down, center it, and pull up an apple-sized piece of clay.

2. Slow the wheel to a moderate speed and open the pot with your right thumb. Then insert two fingers from your left hand into the opening for the first pull up from the bottom to the top. Your left thumb helps shape it from the outside. Use your sponge to add a little water to the sides of the mug with each pull.

3. When you reach the top, push down with the sponge to shape and thicken the lip of the mug.

4. Put your left hand inside the mug for the second pull. Remember to use your sponge to keep water from accumulating on the bottom of the mug. Shape the lip of the mug with the sponge after each pull.

5. After three pulls, shape the mug from the bottom to the top with the wheel at a moderate to slow speed. This mug will be more squat and belled higher at the top than the first mug. With the shape you desire in mind, apply more pressure with your inside hand to bell the mug outward. Press in with your outside hand to complete the rounded shape, then flare the top slightly with more pressure from your inside hand.

6. Continue to work on the shape with the wheel at a moderate to slow speed. Make a ridge about an inch below the lip by pushing out with the left middle finger between the right index and middle fingers, which are pushing in.

7. Shape the mug three or four times, using counterpressure from your inside and outside hands to achieve the shape you are seeking.

8. Once the shaping is finished, smooth the rim with the wet chamois with the wheel at a moderate speed.

Decorating the Mug

1. Use a paintbrush to apply the decorative iron-bearing slip to the mug. (See pages 13 and 14 for instructions on how to make slip.) The slip will add color beneath the glaze of the finished mug. Hold the brush stationary against the mug just below the ridge while the wheel turns slowly.

2. Apply a second band of slip below the first, leaving about ½ inch of space between the two bands.

3. Use a darker shaded slip to apply a third band between the first two bands of slip.

4. To add a decorative ridged band around the mug, take a modeling tool and, pressing lightly, move it from the top to the bottom of the bands of slip while the wheel turns slowly.

5. To further decorate the mug, scratch up and down across the bands of slip with a potter's rib.

6. When you've finished decorating the piece, use the cutting tool to partially separate the mug from the clay mound while the wheel spins at a moderate speed.

7. With the wheel turned off, cut the mug from the clay mound with the wire clay cutter. Carefully set the mug aside to dry.

Style 3
The third style of mug has straight sides, but it begins the same way as the first two.

1. Pull up an apple-sized piece of clay with the wheel at a high speed.

2. Open the clay with your right thumb and pull it up with the fingers of your left hand. Remember to add a little water to the sides with each pull and sponge away water that accumulates in the base of the mug.

3. The second pull up begins the same way with the left hand inserted into the pot to widen it. To create a more linear look for the mug, pull straight up rather than bell the mug. Remember to pull up at a moderate speed and shape at a moderate to slow speed.

4. By the end of the second pull, the mug's shape has begun to differ from the previous mugs. Use more pressure from your inside hand to make the bottom wider, then apply a little more pressure from your outside hand to gently taper it. Remember to shape the lip after each pull.

5. When the third pull is complete, you can see how the mug flares slightly at the base and then tapers toward the top. Use counterpressure from your inside and outside hands to create the shape, pressing in slightly with your outside hand to create the taper.

6. Now the shape can be further refined using a metal potter's rib with a straight edge. Shape and smooth the mug from the bottom to the top and back down.

7. Starting from the top again, apply a little inward pressure right underneath the lip to establish it.

8. Use a wet chamois to smooth the lip.

9. Clean clay off the rib with your sponge after each pass.

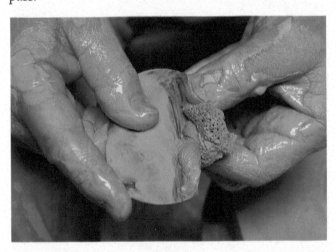

10. Shape the mug three times with the rib.

11. Finish by smoothing the lip with the chamois.

12. Apply light brown slip, starting the first band about a third of the way down the flat expanse of the mug. Remember to keep the wheel at a slow speed for all the decorating steps.

13. Apply a second band of lighter-colored slip about an inch below the first band. Finish by applying a band of darker brown slip between the first two bands.

14. Use the modeling tool to score the side of the mug from top to bottom and back to the top.

15. You can feather the bands of slip up and down with the potter's rib to create an interesting pattern. If you like the effect, there's really no wrong way to decorate your piece.

16. With the wheel at a moderate speed, use the cutting tool to begin to remove the mug from the mound.

17. With the wheel turned off, use the wire clay cutter to finish cutting the mug from the mound. Then set the mug aside to dry.

49

After the mugs have dried to the leather-hard stage, they are ready to be trimmed on the wheel. It takes several hours to a few days to reach the leather-hard stage. At this stage the mugs will hold their shapes if you handle them, but the clay is still somewhat pliable. When they reach that stage, trim them, or cover them with plastic to keep them from drying further.

Quite a bit of clay must be trimmed from the bottom of each mug. The mug on the left is trimmed and the mug on the right is not.

1. Place a mug upside down on the wheel as close to the center as possible, then tap-center it by gently tapping the mug where it is farthest out of center with the wheel at a moderate to high speed.

2. Once the mug is centered, turn off the wheel and secure the mug to the bat with three pieces of clay.

3. Use the loop tool to begin trimming excess clay from the bottom of the mug. Using the large end of the loop tool, hold it against the bottom of the mug firmly enough to peel away a thin layer of clay. Start in the center and move outward.

All trimming should be done with the wheel at a moderate to high speed.

4. Establish a flat bottom.

5. Now use the loop tool to cut in hard at the edge to make the foot rim.

6. Next, hollow out the center of the base.

7. Leave about ¼- to ⅜-inch thickness so you have a rim.

8. It's a trial-and-error process to know when you've cut away enough clay. One way to check is to press down lightly on the clay with the wheel off. If you can feel it move, don't cut any deeper.

9. Sponge the foot rim with the wheel at a moderate to high speed. Stamp the rim or carve your initials into it.

This piece of equipment is called a Giffin Grip; it can be used instead of pieces of clay to secure a piece to a bat and speed up the trimming process. It attaches to the wheel head with tabs. Hold the grip and, with the wheel head turning, pull the three tabs into the middle. The two mug styles with curved sides are trimmed in the same way. The Giffin Grip is used to hold them during trimming.

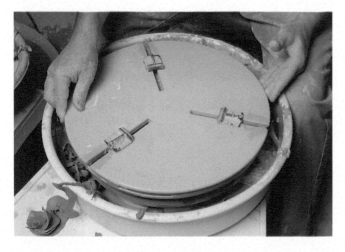

1. Place the first belled mug you made on the Giffin Grip as close as possible to the center. Draw in the tabs by holding the top of the pad and rotating the wheel slowly with the foot pedal. The Giffin Grip centers the piece for you.

2. Use the loop tool to trim excess clay from the bottom of the mug, starting at the inside and moving out. Again, all trimming will be done with the wheel at a moderate to high speed.

3. Trim until the bottom of the mug is flat.

4. Next, trim the edge to make the foot rim.

As with the previous mug, a considerable amount of trimming must be done to establish the foot rim.

5. Now work to hollow the base, still using the loop tool.

Remember to leave enough thickness for the rim.

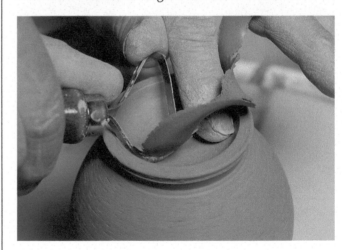

6. Trim the edge of the foot rim.

7. Lightly trim the side of the mug to refine the shape.

8. After you've finished trimming, use your sponge to smooth the foot rim while the wheel spins at a moderate to high speed.

Applying Slip

Slip can be applied on this mug at this stage. It couldn't be applied earlier because of the trimming required.

1. Use a paintbrush held stationary to apply the first band of slip near the middle of the mug while the wheel rotates slowly.

2. Add another band of slip about an inch above the first band.

Making Mugs

3. Add a band of darker slip between the first two bands.

4. Use a toothed metal potter's rib to add detail to the slip.

5. Feather up and down across the bands of slip while the wheel slowly turns. You can feather continuously or leave gaps depending on the desired effect.

6. Remove the mug from the Giffin Grip and set it aside to dry. Drying will take from two days to a week.

Trimming the Second Mug

1. Center the mug in the Giffin Grip and secure it. Begin trimming the base of the mug with the loop tool while the wheel spins at a moderate to high speed.

2. When the base is flat, trim the edge of the mug to establish the foot rim.

3. Carefully smooth the bottom third of the mug with the loop tool.

4. Hollow the base of the mug.

5. Trim the edge of the foot rim. Sponge the foot rim to smooth it.

Adding a Handle

After the mugs are trimmed, the next step is to add handles to them. You'll learn to make pulled handles in two styles.

Pulling a handle that is comfortable and well balanced is a skill that requires much practice and trial and error. Don't be discouraged if initial attempts are unsatisfactory. Continued practice will hone your skills.

Style 1

1. Use this handle for the first mug style. Place newspaper on a flat workspace close to a pan of water. (You won't use the potter's wheel to make the handles.)

2. Shape a large piece of wedged clay into an elongated cone, as shown.

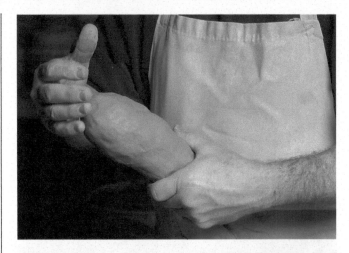

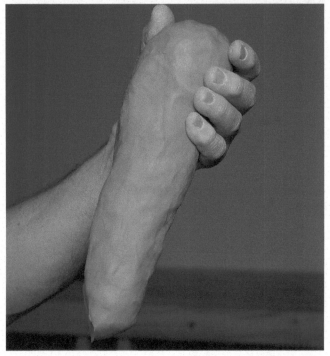

3. Dip your right hand into the pan of water to wet all your fingers.

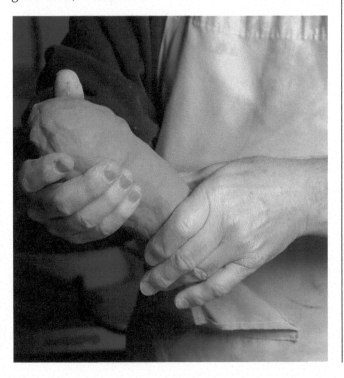

4. Hold the clay in your left hand and place your wet right hand around the clay cone. Begin pulling the clay between the thumb and fingers of your right hand, keeping the left hand still.

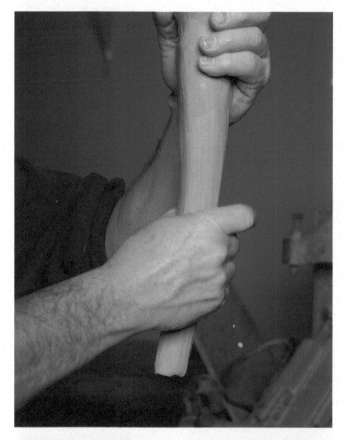

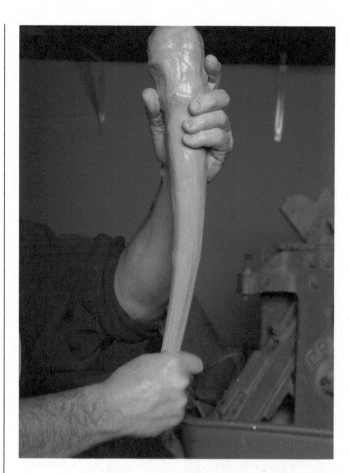

5. Continue pulling and stretching the clay, rewetting your right hand as necessary.

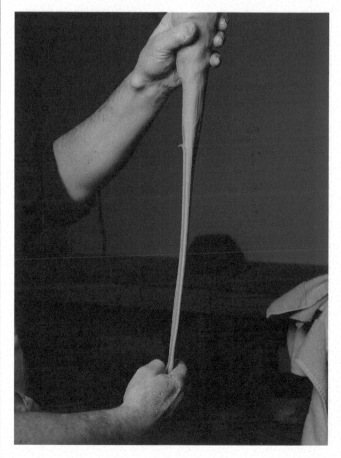

6. Add a groove on the right side of the clay by pressing with your thumb while pulling. Pull two or three times to establish the groove.

7. Now make a second groove on the left side in the same way.

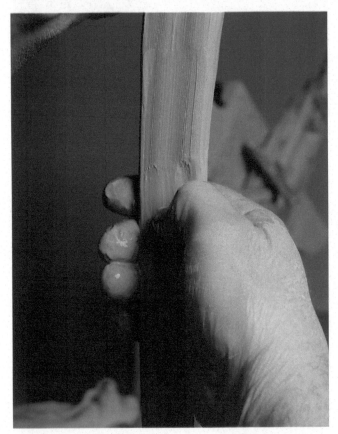

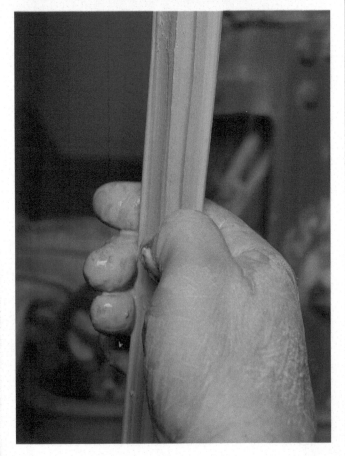

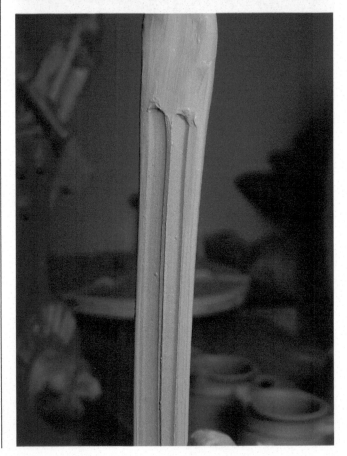

8. Continue working on the grooves until they are fairly pronounced.

9. Now pull the clay between two of your fingers to smooth it.

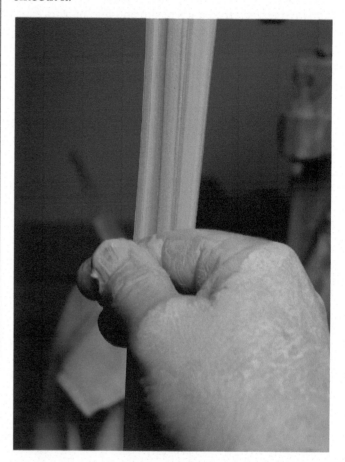

10. Squeeze off 10-inch-long, ¼-inch-thick pieces of the pulled clay to use as handles for the first style of mug. You can do this by pinching the clay between your fingers to "cut" it. Pinch off one piece of clay for each mug. Set the pieces aside.

11. Holding the mug between your legs, use a needle tool to score the mug in a crisscross pattern about halfway between the bands of slip and the top rim, as shown. Add more crisscross scoring at the bottom edge of the slip.

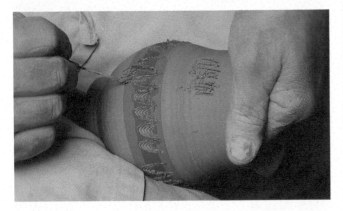

12. Use a brush to apply a thick coat of uncolored slip to the scoring.

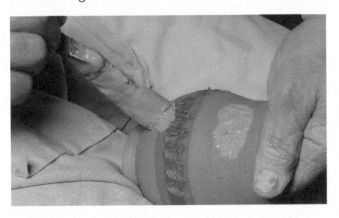

13. Now pick up a handle with the grooves facing you.

14. Flip the handle and work it into the side of the mug at the top scoring with your index finger. Wet your finger, then press and smooth the top of the handle into the mug. (The grooved side of the handle should be facing the slip.)

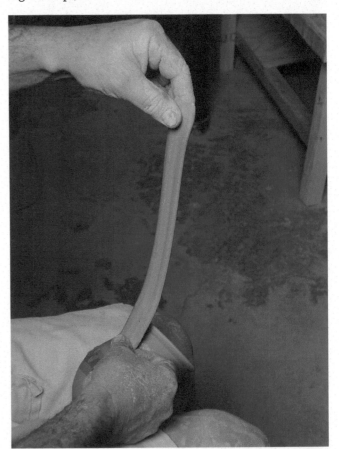

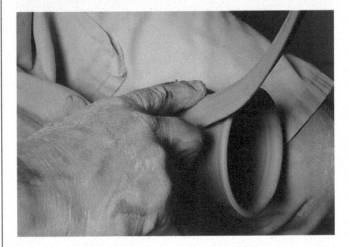

15. Continue to work the handle into the side of the mug at the top scoring. Finish by smoothing it with a wet sponge.

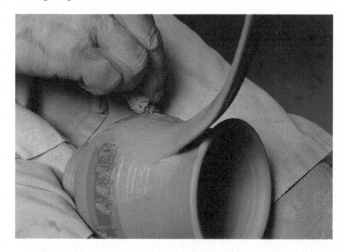

16. Bend the handle and press it into the side of the mug at the bottom scoring.

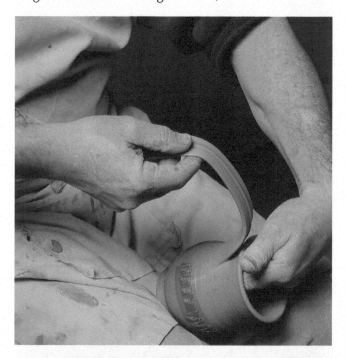

17. Use your index finger to press the handle securely to the side of the mug at the bottom scoring. Pull off the excess handle material.

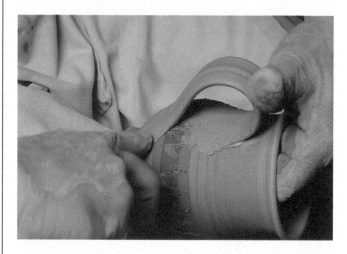

18. Clean and smooth the area with your sponge.

19. Pull off a little piece of clay from the excess material and roll it into a ball about ½ inch in diameter.

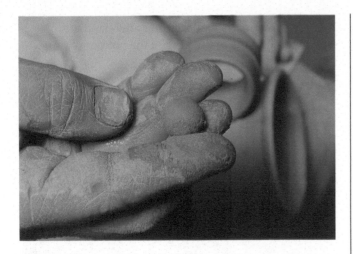

20. Press the ball onto the base of the handle with your thumb. This adds a decorative touch to the handle.

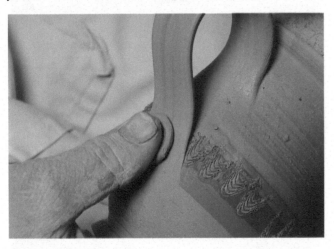

21. You can stamp the mug directly on the clay ball. Your mug is now ready to finish drying before its first firing.

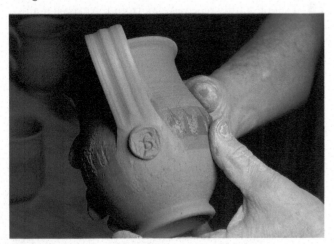

Style 2

You'll make a smaller handle with a thumb hold for the other mugs.

1. Begin by pulling an elongated cone of clay between the thumb and fingers of your right hand.

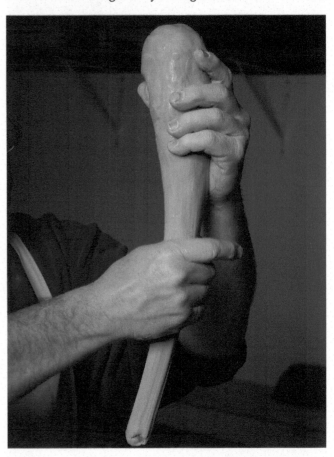

2. Use the fettling knife to cut off handles about 6 to 8 inches in length that taper from about ¾ to ¼ inch thick. You'll use the fettling knife instead of your fingers this time because the thick end of the handle attaches directly to the mug.

3. Set the handles aside.

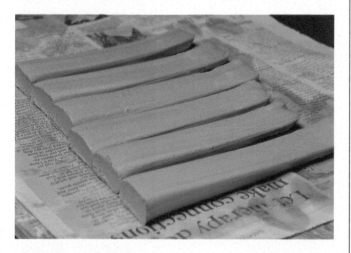

4. Score the mug with the needle tool just below the ridge.

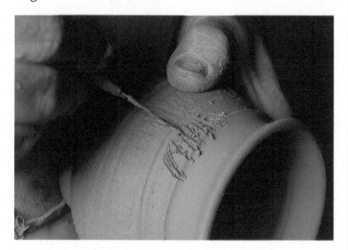

5. Now score it about 1½ inches below the first scoring.

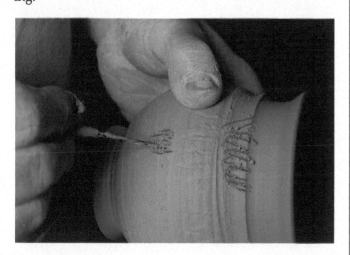

6. Apply a thick layer of uncolored slip to the scoring.

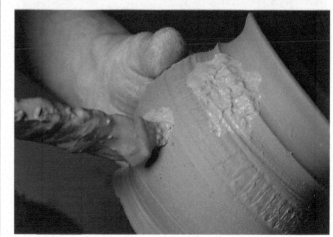

7. Flare the thicker end of the handle by pressing the perimeter of the end between your thumb and finger.

8. Attach it securely to the top scoring using your thumb and fingers.

9. Once the handle is securely attached, hold the mug stationary in your left hand, wet your right hand, and pull the handle between two fingers of your right hand to make it longer. Several passes must be made in order to pull the handle to the correct length and thickness.

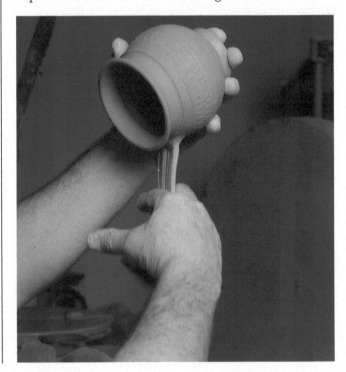

10. Make a small loop in the handle and attach the bottom portion to the bottom scoring. Press it tightly to secure.

11. Cut off the excess handle in a semicircle with the pin tool.

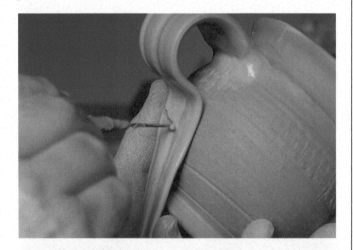

12. Set the mug aside to dry thoroughly. Drying will take from two days to a week.

Adding a Handle with a Thumb Hold

1. First score the mug about an inch below the rim. Score it again about 1½ inches below the first scoring.

2. Apply slip to the scoring.

3. Flare the thicker end of the handle. Place the mug on a table and firmly press the flared end of the handle into the top scoring. It's helpful to press from the inside of the mug with your free hand.

4. With your thumb and index finger, secure the handle and smooth the area where it meets the mug.

5. Once the handle is secure, pick up the mug in your left hand. Wet your right hand and pull the handle between your thumb and fingers to make it longer. Move your fingers while keeping the mug still. Several passes must be made in order to pull the handle to the correct length and thickness.

6. Make a small loop with the handle and press it firmly with your thumb to the bottom scoring.

7. Cut off the excess handle material in a semicircle with the needle tool.

8. Finish your mug by making a thumb hold. Pinch off and roll a small piece of clay into a ball about ½ inch in diameter. Set the ball on a work surface protected by newspaper.

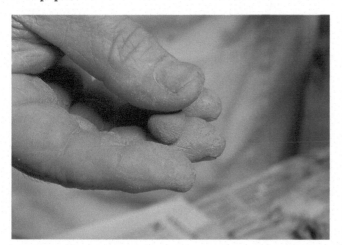

9. Use your index finger to push in the center of the ball and then "smear" one side of the ball.

Making Mugs

10. Score the top of the handle with the needle tool.

11. Dab a small amount of uncolored slip on the scoring.

12. Carefully pick up the thumb hold from the newspaper.

13. Place the thumb hold on the slip with the tapered end facing the mug's rim.

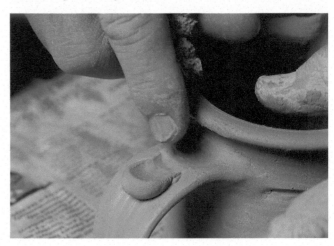

14. Wet your index finger and work in the thumb hold.

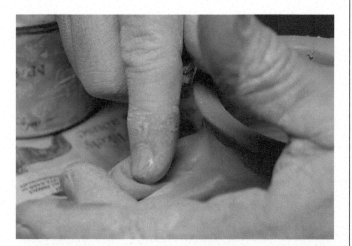

15. Use a sponge to clean up the edges. Set the mug aside to finish drying. The next step is bisque firing, which is covered in chapter 6.

5

Making a Sugar Bowl and Creamer Set

Making this sugar bowl and creamer set teaches a couple of new skills. You'll learn how to make a spout and a lidded pot. You'll use a 1-pound piece of clay to make each piece.

Blocking Clay

You'll need to first cut down a large block of clay into smaller, more manageable portions.

1. Wedge a 7- or 8-pound piece of clay, then block it by dropping it onto a sturdy, flat work surface.

2. Pick up the clay, turn it, and drop it again.

3. Continue this process for all four sides and both ends so you form a rectangular block, as shown.

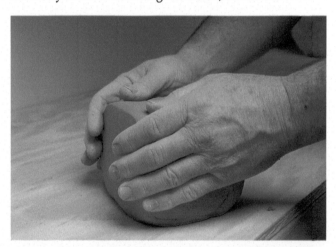

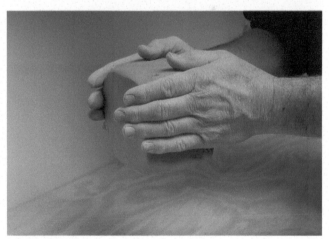

73

4. Once the clay is blocked, you'll use the wire clay cutter to divide it into individual pieces.

5. Cut the block in half horizontally with the wire, pulling the cutter toward you.

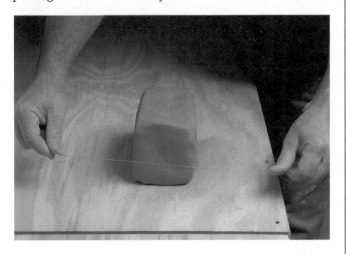

6. After the block is cut in half, turn the whole thing over.

7. Again, cut the block in half horizontally with the wire.

8. Stand the block on one end and cut it horizontally into three sections.

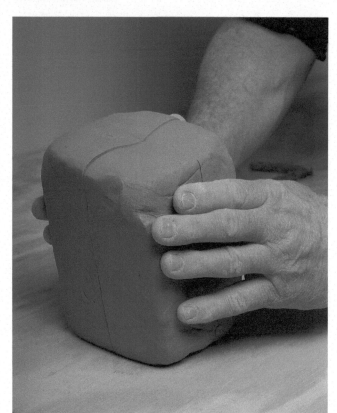

9. Pull apart the pieces you've cut and place one on the scale to see if it weighs 1 pound.

10. If you need to, add small slices of clay to make each segment 1 pound (or remove a bit of clay if it's too heavy).

11. When you've fashioned the clay into 1-pound segments, shape each one with your hands to form a round ball.

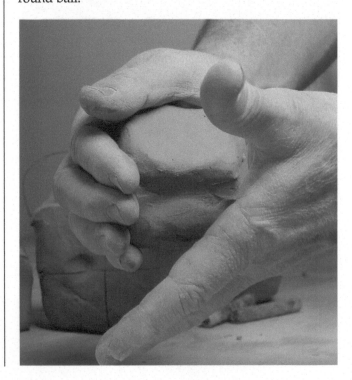

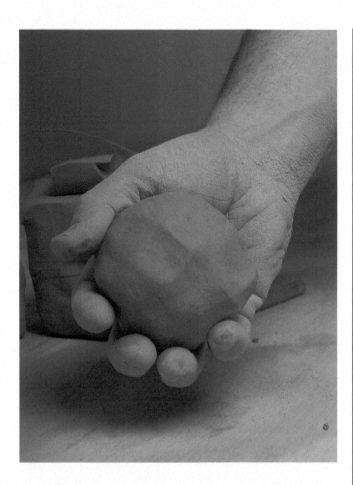

This bat of 1-pound clay balls will be made into three creamers and three sugar bowls.

Making the Cream Pitcher

As with the mugs, clay will be centered and shaped with the wheel at a fast speed. Pull up the pieces with the wheel at a moderate speed, then shape the pieces with the wheel at a moderate to slow speed.

1. Set the clay pieces close to your pottery wheel.

2. Place a clean bat on the wheel and wet it with your sponge. Stop the wheel and place one of the clay balls on the bat as close to the center as possible.

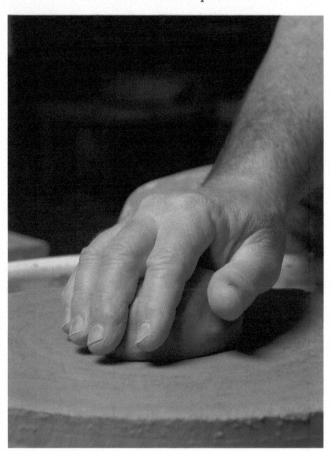

3. Slap the clay to flatten it slightly.

4. Wet your sponge, turn on the wheel, and lubricate the clay.

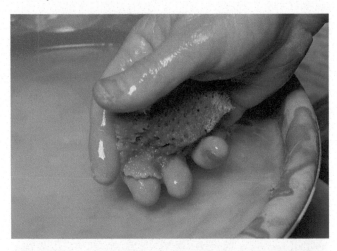

5. Center the clay using a fast wheel speed, keeping the sponge in your left hand to moisten the clay as you push in on it.

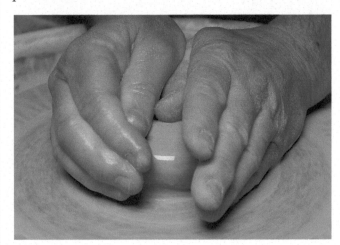

6. Push in until the clay isn't wobbling anymore and you've shaped it into a disk.

7. With the wheel rotating at a moderate speed, begin to open the clay with your right thumb.

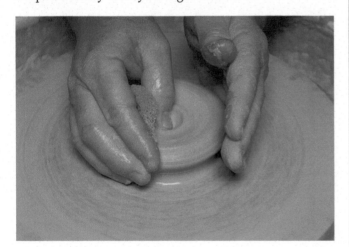

8. Push down with your thumb and move it outward from the center.

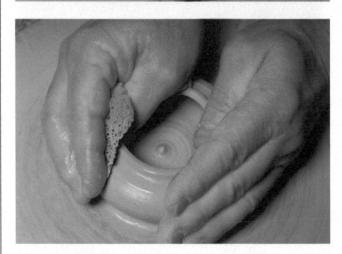

The pot is now ready for the first pull.

9. With your left hand inside and your right hand outside, begin to pull up the pot with the wheel at a moderate speed. Use your sponge to apply a little water to the outside of the pot during each pull.

10. Sponge up excess moisture from the bottom of the pot when necessary.

11. Continue pulling up with your left hand inside and your right hand outside.

12. Because this pot will have a spout, you'll need to make a substantially thicker lip on it by pressing down with your right hand while molding the lip with the thumb and fingers of your left hand.

The thicker lip emerges.

13. On the next pull, continue to shape the pitcher.

14. Work to keep the lip thick by pressing down with your right hand while shaping with your left thumb and fingers.

15. On the final pull, bell out the bottom of the pitcher slightly by applying light pressure with your inside hand. Use the needle tool to measure the thickness of the bottom. The bottom should be about ¼ to ½ inch thick.

You'll use a thin metal potter's rib to make a ridge around the piece.

16. With the wheel on moderate speed, hold the rib in your right hand and apply pressure to the outside of the pot.

17. Sponge the ridge to smooth it.

18. Take one more pass up the outside of the pot to refine the shape of the pitcher.

19. Smooth the lip of the pitcher with the wet chamois.

20. Use the cutting tool to bevel the bottom of the piece while the wheel spins at a moderate speed.

21. Use the sponge to smooth the beveled area.

22. Shape the outside of the pitcher once more.

23. With the wheel on a slow speed, cut a groove into the base with a wooden modeling tool.

24. Stop the wheel and cut the piece from the bat with a wire clay cutter. Keep the wire firmly on the bat as you cut.

Shaping the Spout

The next step in making your cream pitcher is to shape the spout. Shaping will be done with the wheel off.

1. Establish two points with your left thumb and index finger where the spout will be. Hold your fingers about an inch apart.

2. While holding that position with your left hand, begin to form the spout by moving your right index or middle finger back and forth between those two points.

3. Gently squeeze the clay of this curve between your thumb and index finger until it is thinner than the rest of the lip.

4. Keep dipping your fingers in water to keep them wet as you continue to thin and shape the spout.

5. Using the thumb and index finger of your left hand to hold the rim in place, carefully shape the spout with the index finger of your right hand

6. Work the clay until the spout is evenly shaped.

7. Sponge the spout area.

8. Lift the bat off the wheel with the bat lifter.

9. Leave the pitcher on the bat and set it aside to dry to the leather-hard stage (see tip on page 28).

87

Making the Sugar Bowl

The next step is to make the sugar bowl. One thing to remember is that you're trying to match it to the creamer you just made. You'll begin the same way as you did with the pitcher.

1. Wet the bat and place a 1-pound piece of clay as close to the center as possible, flattening it slightly. With the wheel at a moderate to high speed, use your sponge to wet the clay and center it by pushing in with your hands until it no longer wobbles.

2. Open the clay by pressing your right thumb down into it and moving it out from the center.

3. Pull up the pot from the bottom to the top with the left hand inside and the right hand outside. Wet the outside of the pot with your sponge with each pull.

4. Pull up the pot again, keeping a fairly thick rim. Shape the rim by pressing down each time you reach the top of the pot.

5. Bell the bottom of the bowl slightly to match the pitcher on the last pull up.

6. Use the metal potter's rib to make the ridge under the lip of the bowl. Sponge it smooth.

7. You'll need to establish a gallery or ledge where the lid will sit. First make sure the lip is thick and smooth.

8. Hold the sponge in your right hand and use the tip of your left thumb to press down about halfway across the lip while the wheel is moderately rotating.

9. Continue to press down with the tip of your left thumb while supporting the outside of the rim with your right hand, keeping the wheel speed moderate.

10. Once the ledge is established, use the wet chamois to remove particle residue.

11. When the ledge is established, reestablish the shape of the whole piece.

12. Use the cutting tool to bevel the bottom edge.

13. Smooth the beveled edge with the sponge.

14. Use the modeling tool to make an indentation at the base.

To make sure the lid fits, the bowl opening must be measured before it has dried.

15. With the wheel turned off, use calipers to measure the diameter of the opening. Adjust the calipers so they just fit inside the rim. Set the calipers aside; you'll use them later to measure the width of the lid.

16. Lift the bat off the wheel and set the sugar bowl aside to dry.

Making the Lid

You'll make the lid for the sugar bowl by throwing off a mound. A 6- to 8-pound piece of clay is used for the mound.

1. With the wheel at a fast speed and the clay as close to the center of the wheel as possible, begin working it up and down, wetting it with your sponge. Center a plum-sized piece of clay at the top of the mound.

2. Flatten the clay at the top slightly.

3. Make a small opening in the center of the clay to the depth of the first joint of your index finger. This will be the lid's knob.

4. Pull up the clay knob slightly with your two index fingers.

5. With the wheel at a slow to moderate speed, carefully press the clay inward with your fingers to nearly close the opening. This creates a hollow knob.

6. Leave a small air hole at the top until you work on the bottom of the knob.

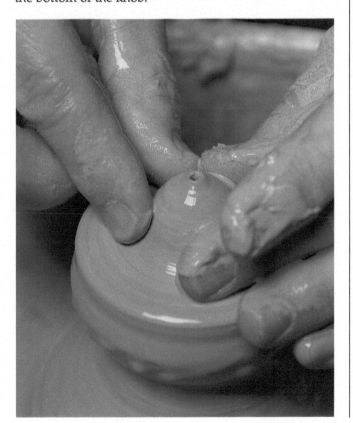

7. Squeeze in until you get the bottom of the knob as thin as you want it, but no thinner than ⅜ inch.

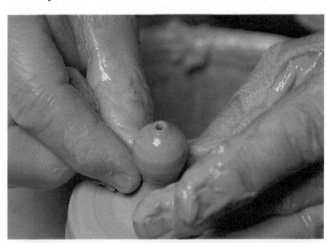

8. Now close the air hole with your index finger and refine the shape of the knob.

9. To finish your lid, you'll need enough clay to make it the same width as the sugar bowl's opening. Push underneath the lid with your thumb to grab about ¾ to 1 inch of clay.

Note: This step might require some trial and error to determine the amount of clay needed.

10. Stretch out the lid and sponge out the water.

11. With the wheel off, compare the width of the lid with the set calipers so that it matches the sugar bowl ledge. If the sizes don't match, you can easily adjust the lid by stretching it out a little if it is not wide enough or by pushing it in slightly to narrow it.

12. Add a groove at the base of the knob with the modeling tool while the wheel slowly rotates.

13. Round it off with your sponge and check once more with the calipers to make sure the lid matches the bowl's ledge.

14. Use the cutting tool to begin separating the lid from the clay mound while the wheel rotates at a moderate speed.

15. With the wheel off, complete the cut with the wire clay cutter.

16. Set the lid on the bat next to the sugar bowl to dry to the leather-hard stage.

Trimming the Lid

Once the pieces have reached the leather-hard stage, in a few hours to a few days, the lid is ready to be trimmed. The creamer and sugar bowl don't need to be trimmed, but you should wipe the bottom edges with a sponge to smooth them.

1. To prepare for trimming, you'll first make a "chuck" out of clay to hold the lid while you're trimming it. (This chuck won't be part of the finished lid or bowl.) Wet the bat and center a 1-pound ball of clay.

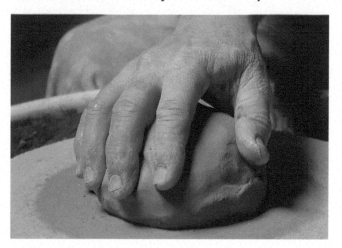

2. With the wheel at a moderate speed, open the clay with your right thumb and make a cylinder that is deep enough and wide enough to accommodate the lid's knob.

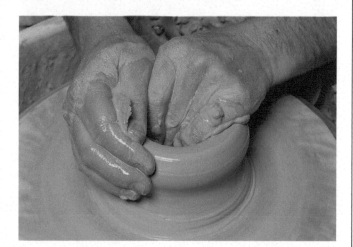

3. Make a thick lip on the cylinder and use calipers to make sure the chuck's opening is the same width as the bowl's ledge.

4. Adjust the clay as necessary so the widths are the same.

5. Let the surface water evaporate off the chuck for about an hour. Then place the lid upside down on the chuck.

6. Tap-center the lid while the wheel is moving at a moderate speed.

7. Use the loop tool to trim the center portion of the lid bottom from the center to the edge. Trim with the wheel at a high speed.

8. Trim until it's flat.

9. Now trim the outer edge from the outside to the base of the middle portion, again with the wheel at a high speed.

10. Use the loop tool to bevel the edge.

11. Sponge the lid to smooth it while the wheel is turning at a moderate to high speed.

12. If you'd like, you can cut out an opening for a sugar spoon. Remove the lid from the chuck and roughly outline the shape with a craft knife.

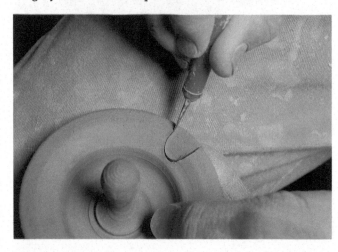

13. Then cut through the outline and remove the slice of clay.

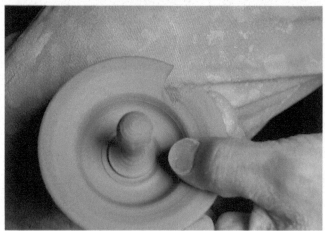

14. Flatten the area of the lid that will sit on the bowl ledge.

15. Place the lid on the sugar bowl and set both aside to dry. Drying takes from two days to a week.

Adding a Handle to the Pitcher

Just as for the mugs, you'll make a pulled handle for the cream pitcher.

1. Stretch the elongated cone using plenty of water. Work the clay up and down. Set it on a newspaper and cut off a length 6 to 8 inches long and about 1 inch wide. The clay should taper from about ¾ to ¼ inch. Continue to work the larger piece of clay and cut off one length for each handle you will make.

2. On the side of the creamer opposite the spout, score the outside of the piece at the top and bottom.

You will score more at the top to accomodate the wider part of the handle.

3. Apply a thick coat of uncolored slip to the scoring.

4. Pick up one of the lengths of clay and flare the thicker end. Firmly attach the flared end to the slip at the top of the pitcher.

5. Work the handle end into the pitcher with your thumb and fingers.

6. When the attachment is firmly made, pick up the piece in your left hand with the handle hanging down.

7. Wet your right hand and move it over the clay to stretch the handle another 2 or 3 inches. Curve your hand around the handle to shape the back and sides as you pull your hand over the clay.

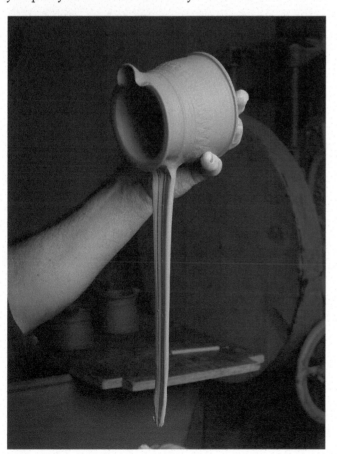

8. If you'd like, you can indent the handle with your thumb as you pull.

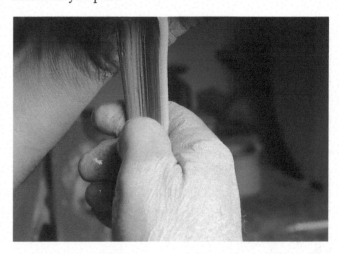

9. Turn the handle and attach it firmly to the slip at the bottom of the pitcher.

10. Cut off the excess in a semicircle with the needle tool.

11. Sponge off the cut end and firmly push in the handle at the base and top with your index finger. Set the pitcher aside to dry.

6

Firing and Glazing

Bisque firing, glazing, and glaze firing are the final steps in making pottery. To save time and money, it's best to fire and glaze a number of pieces at one time—as many as your kiln will hold.

A pot must dry from the leather-hard stage (see tip on page 28) to the bone-dry stage before it can be bisque fired, which prepares the piece to be glazed. Drying a piece to the bone-dry stage takes from two days up to a week, depending on humidity. Drying in less than two days is not recommended because if a pot dries too quickly, it can crack.

A bone-dry pot will have a completely bleached look and no dampness will be visible. Because pots dry from the top down, you should turn your pots over to see if they are completely dry. A pot that is not completely dry can explode during firing.

The bottom of the mug on the left still shows some dampness and must dry longer before firing. The mug on the right is bone dry and ready to be fired. Pieces can be kept indefinitely at the bone-dry stage before firing.

1. After you have filled your kiln, close the lid.

2. Follow the operating directions for your kiln. For the bisque firing, the temperature must reach a temperature of cone 07 or about 1789 degrees Fahrenheit. It should take about 10 to 12 hours. Turn off the kiln when the temperature is reached.

Firing and Glazing

Filling the Kiln

If you're firing your pieces yourself, fill the kiln with your bone-dry pieces. Most kilns can fire more than one layer of pots at a time. If you are firing more than one layer, arrange your pieces by height before filling the kiln. Save your tallest pieces for the top shelf. Use posts and shelves that were designed for your kiln. To hold up the shelf, choose posts that are at least ½ inch taller than the tallest pot that will be beneath them. Place the post in the kiln before placing the pots. You'll need four to six posts to hold up two half shelves or one full shelf. In general, posts are placed in the corners of rectangular shelves and under the outside of circular shelves. When placing two half shelves, the two posts on the side where the shelves meet can hold up both half shelves.

After you've placed your posts, fill the bottom layer of the kiln, placing the pieces as close together as possible. It is okay for pieces to touch each other, the posts, or the walls during bisque firing, but they shouldn't touch any heating elements. Once you've completely filled the bottom level, carefully place the full shelf or half shelves on top of the posts. If you're using more than one shelf, position the posts for each shelf in the same place so that the posts carry the weight.

3. When the kiln has cooled to a temperature of 250 degrees or lower, it can be opened. Follow the manufacturer's directions to secure the lid in the opened position. Let pieces cool to room temperature.

Cone Ratings

Kilns are fired not just to a temperature but to a "cone" level, which includes firing time as well as temperature. Cone ratings range from 022 to 10, with cone 10 being the hottest.

Don't let the zeroes fool you. A cone rating of 07 is much cooler than a cone rating of 7. When heating up the kiln at a medium rate, also known as a "ramping rate," a cone 7 rating reaches 2262 degrees Fahrenheit while a cone 07 reaches just 1789 degrees.

4. Remove items from the kiln.

5. Set pieces aside for glazing.

Each piece must be waxed in certain places before it is glazed. Wax resists glaze so that when a piece is dipped in glaze, the portion that is waxed keeps the glaze from adhering.

The bottom of all pieces must be coated in wax. Because glaze melts when it is fired, the bottom of a pot would fuse to the kiln shelf during firing if it were glazed.

Because the sugar bowl is fired with its lid on, the areas of the bowl and lid that are in contact can't have glaze on them or they will fuse together during the glaze firing. You'll wax those areas and the bottom of both pieces.

1. Dip a narrow brush into a container of wax and wipe most of the wax off on the container's side.

2. Apply a thin coat of wax to the inside edge of the lip rim and the lid shelf.

Tip: Be careful not to drip wax on other areas of the pot or the drops of wax will keep glaze from sticking.

3. Make sure the wax thoroughly covers the areas the lid will touch.

4. Next, hold the sugar bowl by the top edge and dip the bottom into the wax to just below the groove near the base.

5. Lift up the bowl and let the excess wax drip back into the wax container. Set the bowl aside on a work surface covered with newspaper. Do not place the bowl upside down because the wax could run on areas where you don't want it.

Firing and Glazing

109

6. Use a brush to apply a thin coat of wax to the flat part on the inside of the lid.

7. Make sure to coat it thoroughly.

8. Wax the edge of the lid, including the spoon slot.

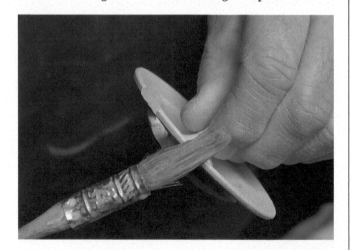

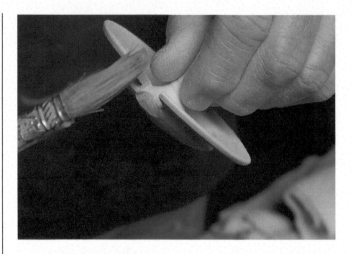

9. Place the lid back on the sugar bowl.

10. Now dip the bottom of the cream pitcher into the container of wax to just below the groove near the base.

11. Pull the pitcher from the wax and let the excess wax drip back into the container. Set the pitcher right side up on a work surface covered with newspaper.

12. The bottom of the bowl must stay free of glaze, too. Use a slightly wider brush to apply wax onto the bottom of the bowl.

13. Make sure to coat the entire surface of the bottom.

14. Use the flat edge of the brush to apply wax to the bottom edge.

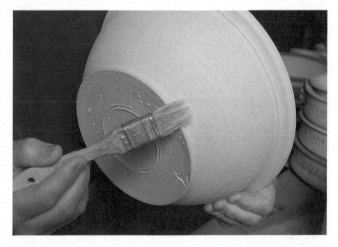

15. To wax the mugs, hold one by the rim and dip it into the wax about three-quarters of the way up the foot ring.

16. Pull the mug out of the wax and shake off the excess. When it stops dripping, turn it over and use the narrow brush to fill in any area on the inside of the ring that didn't get waxed. Set the mug aside right side up.

17. The other two mugs are waxed in the same way. Dip each into the wax about three-quarters of the way up the foot ring, pull out and shake off the excess wax, and brush wax onto any area inside the ring that wasn't coated.

Be careful to not get the wax on any part you want glazed.

Note: The wax will remain tacky, but it will be ready to accept glaze in about five minutes. You can set aside a waxed piece indefinitely before glazing.

Adding glaze and firing your stoneware gives it strength and density and makes it impervious to water. The clay and glaze used must be fired to their maximum temperatures so they "mature" and completely develop. An improperly fired or underfired piece will be porous and not fit for use.

Glazes melt when they are fired. If you want your stoneware pottery to be dinnerware safe, the glaze you use must be fired to at least cone 5 or 6. The cone rating is an indication of temperature that includes firing time. All the glazes on all the pieces you fire at any one time must have the same rating.

Glazes settle between uses. Make sure they're thoroughly stirred before use. For the projects in this book, three different colors of glaze will be used to create different effects on the finished pieces. When you purchase glaze, pick out colors you think will complement each other.

Assemble your glazes before beginning. Shown are a 2-quart pitcher filled with a saturated iron (dark red) glaze and plastic containers, each about 12 to 15 inches in diameter and 4 to 6 inches deep, filled with, from the left, saturated iron glaze, blue ash glaze, and iron red glaze. The smaller plastic container holds water that is used to clean off a stirring paddle or stick. Because they settle quickly, glazes should be stirred frequently.

1. Use an old towel to dust off each piece before dipping.

2. Stir the iron red glaze.

3. To glaze the straight-sided mug, hold it by the rim and carefully dip it into the glaze to the top of the handle.

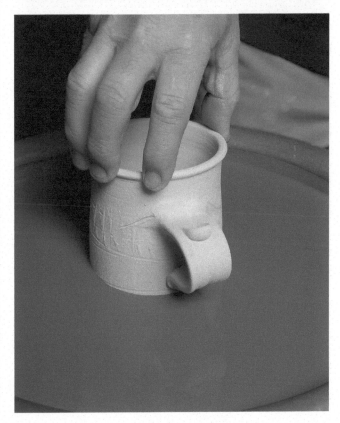

Firing and Glazing

The mug is submerged until the glaze just covers the top of the handle.

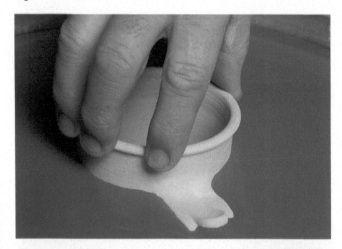

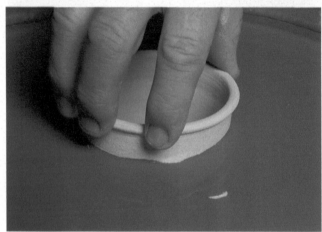

4. Keep the mug in the glaze for about 7 seconds, then pull it out and shake off the excess glaze over the glaze container.

5. Some glaze will bead on the bottom of the mug where it was waxed. You'll clean it later, but for now, set the mug aside right side up on a newspaper-covered work surface.

6. Dust off the shorter round mug and dip it into the glaze to the top of the handle.

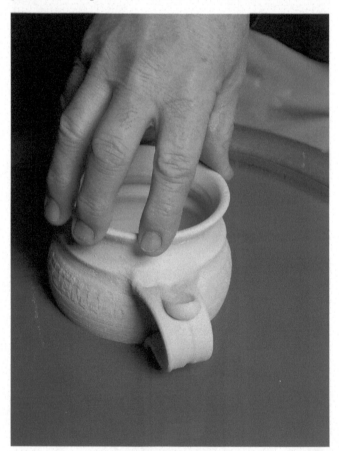

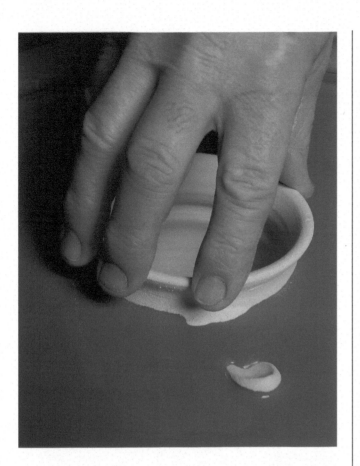

7. Hold the mug in the glaze about 7 seconds then pull it out and shake off the excess glaze. Set it right side up on a newspaper-covered work surface.

8. Dip the taller round mug into the blue ash glaze until the handle is mostly covered.

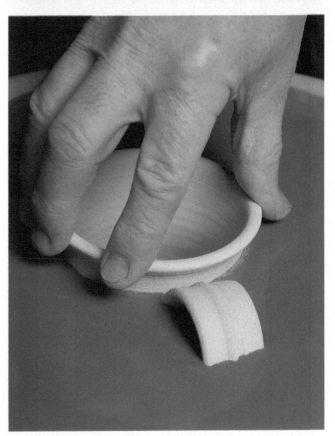

9. After 7 seconds, pull the mug from the glaze and shake off the excess glaze. Set the mug right side up on a newspaper-covered work surface.

10. Glaze takes about a minute to dry. After you've dipped your mugs in their first color, you'll clean the glaze from where it has beaded on the waxed bottoms.

11. Use your sponge and water to clean the excess glaze from the bottom of each of the three mugs.

12. Next, glaze the inside of the mugs in a darker shade. Take the pitcher of dark red glaze and pour it into the first mug until it is about three-quarters full.

13. Pour out the glaze while rotating the mug so that the entire inside and rim is covered with glaze. Hold the mug over the container of glaze until the excess glaze stops dripping.

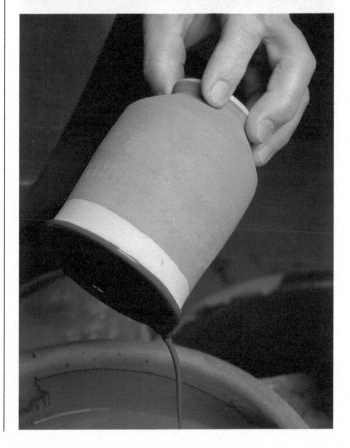

119

14. While the inside glaze is still wet, hold the foot rim of the mug and dip it into the blue ash glaze to the mug handle, overlapping the outside glazes by about ½ inch. Hold the mug in the glaze for about 7 seconds, then pull it out and shake it off.

15. The three colors of glaze are visible. Set the mug aside.

16. Glaze the shorter round mug in the same way, pouring dark red glaze into it until about three-quarters full and rotating the mug while emptying it to swirl the glaze completely around the inside and rim.

17. Plunge the mug up to the top of the handle into the blue ash glaze, overlapping the glazes by about ½ inch, and hold for about 7 seconds.

18. Remove the mug from the glaze and shake out the excess. Set the mug aside.

19. You can finish glazing the third mug just a little differently, using just two colors of glaze instead of three. Fill the mug about three-quarters full with the dark red glaze.

20. Pour out the glaze while swirling the mug. Shake off the excess glaze.

21. Now dip the mug back into the dark red glaze so that the outside glazes overlap by about ½ inch.

22. Pull the mug out of the glaze after about 7 seconds and shake off the excess.

23. Set the mug aside.

1. Next you'll glaze the cream pitcher. First dust it with an old towel. Holding the pitcher by the rim, dip it into the iron red glaze until the handle is nearly covered.

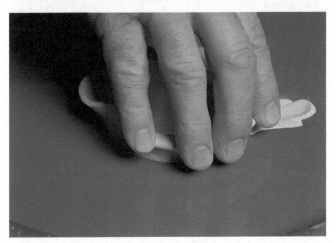

2. After about 7 seconds, lift the pitcher from the glaze and shake it to remove excess glaze.

3. Glaze will bead on the waxed bottom. Set the pitcher aside.

4. Dust the sugar bowl, then dip it into the iron red glaze to just above the ridge and hold it for about 7 seconds.

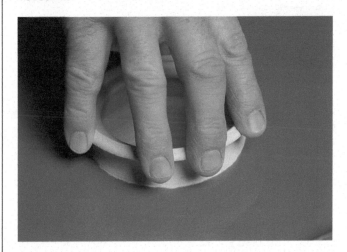

5. Lift the bowl from the glaze, shake off the excess, and set it aside.

6. Use the sponge to clean glaze from the bottom of the cream pitcher and the sugar bowl.

7. Dust the lid with an old towel. Because you're dipping the entire lid, place it in dipping tongs and submerge it into the blue ash glaze. You could also dip it by holding it on the waxed edge with your fingers.

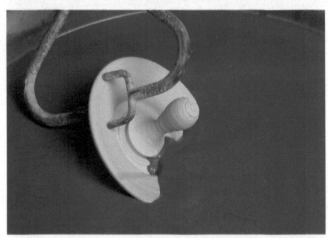

8. After 7 seconds, lift the lid from the glaze and shake off the excess. If any portion isn't covered with glaze, retouch it with a dab of glaze.

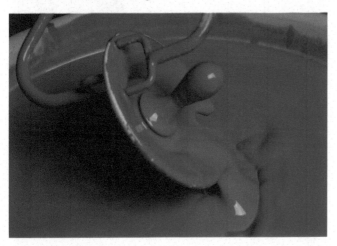

9. Set the lid aside.

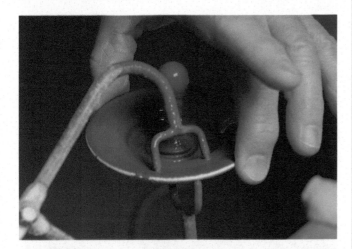

10. Dust the cream pitcher, and fill it about three-quarters full with dark red glaze.

11. Pour out the glaze while swirling the pitcher so that the entire inside and top edge are coated with glaze. Allow the excess glaze to drip from the pitcher.

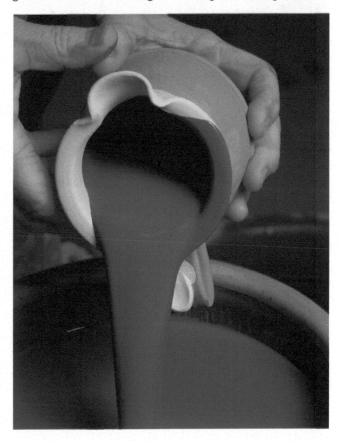

12. Then, holding it by the bottom rim, dip the pitcher into the blue ash glaze so that the top of the handle is covered and the outside glazes overlap by about ½ inch.

13. Pull the pitcher from the glaze and shake it to remove the excess. Set the pitcher aside.

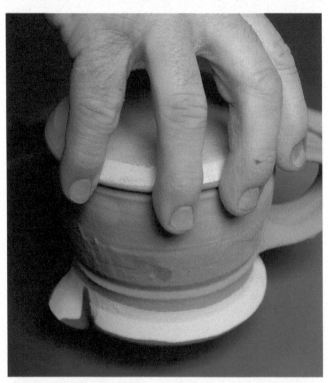

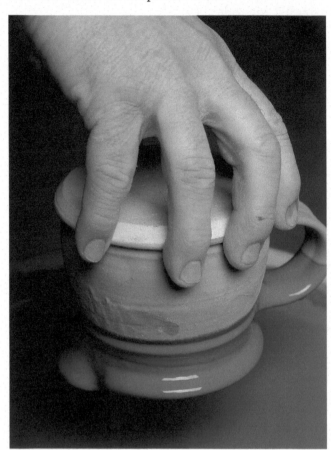

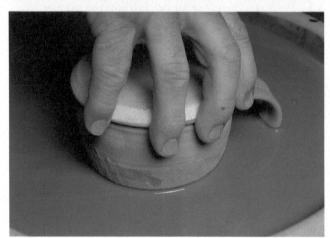

14. Fill the sugar bowl about three-quarters full with dark red glaze.

15. Pour out the glaze while swirling the bowl to coat the inside and top edge with glaze. Shake off the excess glaze.

16. Dip the sugar bowl into the blue ash glaze to just below the ridge, overlapping the glazes by about ½ inch.

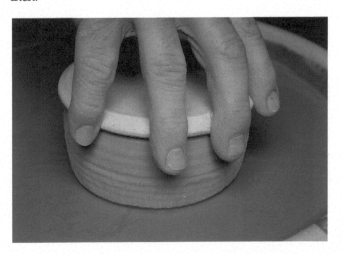

17. After about 7 seconds, pull it out and shake it off.

18. Some glaze will bead on the waxed top of the bowl. Set the bowl aside for at least a minute until the glaze dries.

19. Sponge off the glaze from the waxed portion of the bowl.

20. Sponge glaze off the waxed portion of the lid.

21. Apply a dab of glaze to the rough area of glaze where the lid sat while the glaze dried.

22. Place the lid on the sugar bowl and set it aside. It is now ready for the glaze firing.

1. Remember to clean the bowl thoroughly with a towel before dipping.

2. Because of its size, you'll need to dip the bowl a little differently. Find a container wide enough and deep enough to accommodate the bowl. Our potter is using a plastic trash can, but for the hobbyist a smaller container, such as a 5-gallon bucket, could work.

3. Holding the top edges, dip the bowl into the dark red glaze so that three-quarters of the outside is covered with the glaze.

4. Hold the bowl in the glaze for about 7 seconds, then lift and shake off the excess glaze. Set the bowl aside.

5. You'll use the same process to dip another bowl into blue ash glaze. Dip it into the glaze three-quarters of the way up the outside of the bowl.

Firing and Glazing

129

6. Remove the bowl from the glaze, shake off the excess glaze, and set the bowl aside.

7. When the glaze has dried, sponge off the glaze from the waxed bottom of the first bowl.

8. Use a pitcher of dark red glaze to fill the bowl about three-quarters full.

9. Empty the bowl while rotating it so the glaze covers the entire inside and top rim. Shake the bowl to remove excess glaze.

10. Holding it by the base, dip the bowl into the blue ash glaze about an inch past the rim so the outside glazes overlap by about ½ inch.

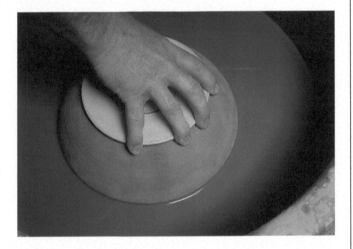

11. Lift the bowl from the glaze after about 7 seconds and shake off the excess glaze.

12. Set the bowl aside.

13. Sponge glaze off the waxed bottom of the second bowl.

14. You'll use iron red glaze to finish this bowl. Fill to about three-quarters full.

15. Swirl the bowl to empty the glaze and coat the inside.

16. Shake the bowl to remove excess glaze.

17. Hold the bowl by its base and dip it into the iron red glaze to about an inch below the rim, overlapping the glazes.

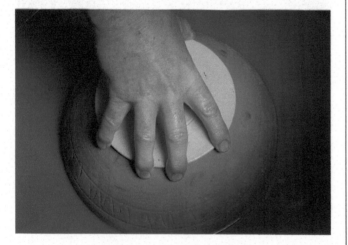

18. Pull the bowl out after 7 seconds, shake, and set aside to dry.

Once all of your pots have been glazed, it's time for the glaze firing. If you've chosen cone 5 glazes, they will be fired to a temperature of about 2167 degrees Fahrenheit. Cone 6 glazes are fired to a temperature of about 2232 degrees. Follow the directions for your kiln and program it so the temperature rises moderately. It should take about 10 to 12 hours to reach the cone 5 or 6 temperature.

Although pots are ready to be fired within minutes of being glazed, they can be held indefinitely. You can fire just a few pieces, especially when beginning, to make sure you've made your pots properly and they don't break during firing, but it is more economical to fire a full kiln.

1. When you put a piece in the kiln for the glaze firing, place it against the wall and then back it off less than a quarter of an inch so there is no contact between the pot and the wall.

Note: If you are firing more than one layer of pots, remember to place the posts that will hold up the full and half shelves before positioning the pots in the kiln.

2. For efficiency, try to fit pieces in closely but make sure they do not touch each other.

3. To ensure pieces are not touching, touch them to each other and then pull them back about ¼ inch. Pots that are touching can fuse together during firing.

Firing and Glazing

133

4. Once the kiln is filled, it can be fired. Look at your pots to make sure none are touching each other, the kiln walls, or the posts. Close the lid. Follow the directions for your kiln and fire to a cone 5 or 6 temperature, depending on your glaze.

5. When the kiln has cooled to a temperature of no higher than 250 degrees, open the lid. Let the pieces cool to room temperature.

6. Carefully take the glazed pots out of the kiln.

7. Just one step remains. Sand the bottom of each piece with 80-grit sandpaper so that it doesn't scratch any surface on which it may be placed.

134

8. Sand the bottom of each mug.

9. Sand the bottoms of the sugar bowl and creamer.

Remember to wash your finished pieces with warm water and mild dish detergent before use. Your stoneware is now microwave and dishwasher safe and ready for you to enjoy.

135

Resources

American Art Clay Co., Inc. (AMACO)
800-374-1600
www.amaco.com
Online only

American Ceramic Supply Co.
2442 Ludelle Street
Fort Worth, TX 76105
866-535-2651
www.americanceramics.com

Axner Pottery Supply
490 Kane Court
Oviedo, FL 32765
800-843-7057
www.axner.com

Bailey Ceramic Supply
62-68 Ten Broeck Avenue
Kingston, NY 12401
800-431-6067
www.baileypottery.com

Ceramic Supply Pittsburgh
412-489-5240
www.ceramicsupplypittsburgh.com

Kentucky Mudworks
800 Floyd Drive Suite 110
Lexington, KY 40505
859-389-9681
www.kentuckymudworks.com

Laguna Clay
www.lagunaclay.com

New Mexico Clay
3300 Girard Boulevard NE
Albuquerque, NM 87107
800-781-2529
www.nmclay.com

About the Experts

Mark and Huynh Mai Fitzgerald

The ongoing rhythm of producing our pottery fills us with a deep sense of satisfaction. We feel very fortunate to be able to live a lifestyle that allows us to maintain a great deal of control over our daily activities. As often as not, these activities in the studio eat up far more of our time than a conventional 9–5 job would. However, the trade-off is well worth it. We are able to see the fruits of our labor on a daily basis, and that is richly rewarding.

We use stoneware as our primary material for forming our pots. This forming is done either on a potter's wheel or using slab-building techniques. Some of the pieces are altered in shape, and handles, which can be either decorative or functional, are added. We then use a combination of wood-ash glazes along with slips, underglazes, and several high-fire feldspathic glazes for surface treatment. The pieces are then fired in a large kiln to nearly 2400 degrees Fahrenheit in what is called a "reduction" atmosphere. This heat and atmosphere combine with the clay and glaze materials to render the finished pieces with their particular colors and surface textures.

Form is of primary importance to us; however, we feel that our pieces must also function well for their intended purposes. For this reason, we take special care with our pots to make sure that the spouts pour, the lids fit, handles are comfortable and balanced, and that all of the requirements of function are met.

We draw our influences from the pots of the early twentieth century made by the likes of Bernard Leach and Shoji Hamada, two pioneers of the studio pottery movement of that era. Organic forms and colors in nature also inspire us. Our work makes no attempt to declare any bold statements or break any new frontiers. Rather, it is the quiet simplicity achieved by carrying on a centuries-old tradition that gives our work its subtle beauty.

It is our hope that the enjoyment we get out of creating our work is somehow transferred to those who choose to own and use our pieces in their daily lives.

We have been married and working as studio partners for over twenty-five years. From 1976 to 1980 we worked under the guidance of Henry Okamoto at Clay Art Center in Port Chester, New York.

While there, we developed technical proficiency in wheel throwing as well as hand building and glaze formulation and application. We also learned the necessary skills of kiln building and firing and acquired the how-to knowledge of the daily operations of a professional studio. Each of us has migrated to areas of production that we feel best meet our individual strengths and interests. Mark does the majority of the materials preparation, wheel throwing, and firing. Huynh Mai concentrates on hand building and glazing. These tasks will often overlap, and many of our pieces result from both our efforts.

From 1980 to the present, we have owned and operated Fitzgerald Pottery in central Pennsylvania. We have exhibited in many of the highest-ranking juried art shows in the United States, and our work is carried in many fine shops and galleries throughout the country.

—M. F. and H. M. F.